Monographic Journals of the Near East   *Syro-Mesopotamian Studies* 4/4 (April 1988)

QRAYA MODULAR REPORTS, No. 1:

EARLY SOUNDINGS

by

Kay Simpson

ABSTRACT

Tell Qraya is a small mound north of Al 'Ashara (ancient Terqa), with an extensive Late Uruk occupation, no evidence of third millennium settlement, and reoccupation during the first half of the second millennium. This fascicle describes the first three seasons of excavation, presents a preliminary analysis of artifacts recovered, and details the stratigraphic history of the site.

Table of Contents

ISBN: 0-89003-050-2

LIST OF FIGURES

LIST OF TABLES

The manuscript of this fascicle was prepared by the author in 1985. The editors regret the subsequent delay in publication, which resulted from causes beyond their control.

1. Introduction

by

Giorgio Buccellati and Marilyn-Kelly Buccellati

1.1   History of the Excavations at Qraya

In 1977 the Joint Expedition to Terqa initiated a program of regional survey of the Middle Euphrates floodplain in the vicinity of Tell 'Ashara, ancient Terqa. Wachtang Djobadze and Olivier Rouault conducted a reconnaisance survey of the easily observable mounds along the river basin from the mouth of the Khabur river to the Syrian-Iraqi border.

This survey was followed in 1978 by an intensive foot survey from 'Ashara westward to the Syrian desert escarpment, for a total of 19 km^2, and in 1979 by an intensive car survey within a 600 km^2 quadrant centered on Tell 'Ashara. The intensive survey of 1978 and 1979 was conducted by Kay Simpson, who presented the results of her research in her 1983 Ph.D. dissertation at the University of Arizona in Tucson (Simpson 1983); a revised version of this work will be published as part of the Terqa Final Reports.

During their initial survey of 1977, Djobadze and Rouault called to our attention the impending danger that was facing the nearby site of Qraya. Upon closer inspection, it was immediately realized that there was an important component of Uruk period material at the site. While the tell had been noticed before (e.g., Kupper 1950:112), its specific archaeological significance had not been fully realized.

The presence of a Protoliterate settlement in the immediate vicinity of Terqa was of particular interest to us because, from all indications we had at the time (and still have today), occupation at Terqa did not precede the early third millennium B.C. It appeared therefore that the Qraya settlement, because of its immediate proximity to Terqa, might represent a direct antecedent to the later urban development at Terqa itself. This consideration, plus the realization that no other sites of that period were known for the Middle Euphrates (Ramadi, a Protoliterate tell near Mari about which see below, 2.1, was discovered later), induced us to ask the Directorate General of Antiquities and Museums for a special permit to conduct excavations there. Given the imminent danger of destruction by the local villagers (much of the upper levels, of the Old Babylonian or Khana period had already been bulldozed away), we stressed the need for immediate, urgent action at the site. With the customary efficiency and spirit of cooperation, the permit was received within a matter of days, and we diverted some of our resources from the Terqa excavations to undertake a small sounding at Qraya, under the direction of William R. Shelby. Similar soundings were continued in the following two years, under the direction of Kay Simpson: it is on these first three seasons of soundings that she reports in this publication. To her we wish to express here our warm appreciation for the skill and determination with which she pursued both the excavations and the preparation of the material for publication, even at a time when she was otherwise heavily involved with her primary work, the Khana regional survey.

These preliminary soundings had proven that the significance of Qraya was considerably greater than just in terms of providing the earliest stage of occupation in the "greater Terqa" region. The thick deposit of Protoliterate material, the nature of the artifactual finds, the strategic location in terms of the diffusion of Uruk period sites in the North (the results from Habuba Kabira, Kannas and Malatya have been published in the meantime)—all of this indicated that continued excavations at Qraya were very much needed.

A first major step in this direction was taken in 1981. In the Fall of that year Daniel Shimabuki undertook a six-week excavation at the site, which was followed by a protracted study period at the Terqa headquarters lasting until the Spring of 1984. The excavations were sponsored by IIMAS — The International Institute for Mesopotamian Area Studies, with the additional support of resources made available by Shimabuku through a Fulbright Research Fellowship which he was holding at the time. He brought to Qraya a special familiarity with Uruk period material due to his previous experience at a major contemporary site in Khuzestan, Chogha Mish (see Shimabuku 1978). A brief preliminary report of his work at Qraya is in press for the *Annales Archeologiques Arabes de Syrie,* while a fuller report is in preparation for a forthcoming issue of the *Qraya Modular Reports.*

The major new insight which resulted from his expanded work at the site was a clearer delineation of specific architectural phases, the recovery of seal impressions on "bullae" and jar sealings, and the realization through a series of test soundings that the ancient settlement extended much beyond the present limits of the mound, in areas which are today under cultivation. We are greatly indebted to Shimabuku for the painstaking laboratory work which he carried out on the Qraya material during a long year spent in the Syrian countryside, and which will prove to be of extreme interest when published.

In 1984 work at the site continued under the direction of Steven Reimer, who had already worked with Shimabuku in 1981. Reimer proposed a long term project for excavations at Qraya, aimed at extending the horizontal exposure of the Protoliterate strata. His first results are briefly summarized below, and they promise much for the future. We are grateful to him for the spirit of initiative which he has demonstrated in assuming the responsibility of field director for the probject, in securing additional funding, and in coordinating a small but very capable staff. The Ph.D. dissertation on which he is currently working will present in systematic fashion the materials and conclusions from his current excavations.

1.2   Significance

Started as a salvage project of what was perceived to be an early historical appendage of greater urban Terqa, the excavations at Qraya have proven to be of considerably more importance than just in terms of a local perspective. The main reason for this lies in the unique constellation of factors present in the evidence recovered there: these have led us to suggest the possibility of a new understanding not only of early Syrian urban history, but of the larger perspective of Sumerian civilization. This new interpretation has a direct bearing on the age-long discussion concerning the function of one of the most ubiquitous types of vessels ever, the beveled rim bowl. But beyond that, it sheds light on some fundamental aspects of early trade, on subsistence patterns and on the nature of early Sumerian expansion to the North.

The main arguments in favor of this interpretation are to be published elsewhere (Buccellati forthc.; they were first hinted at in Buccellati 1977:32). Briefly summarized, the results as proposed in that article are as follows.

Qraya represents a seeming detour in an Uruk period diffusion of settlements which went otherwise north along the Tigris (see Abu al-Soof 1985) and then went across the upper Khabur plains, from Hamukar to Brak and Habuba in modern day Syria (there are in fact no Uruk period sites along the Euphrates south of Qraya and Ramadi until the southernmost Iraqi sites). The detour south along the Khabur to Qraya (and Ramadi) would not seem to have been suggested by agricultural reasons, since the northern Khabur plains provide much better opportunities for farming. Nor was Qraya (or Ramadi, for that matter) a station on a route leading elsewhere, since a more direct route to the big bend of the Euphrates is available from the upper Khabur triangle. Now, if we look for local resources which may have been a target for the detour, one seems to emerge which has been completely ignored so far in the literature, and yet must have been of primary importance for the newly developing urban communities—salt. This commodity was greatly needed in the newly expanding urban setting not only as an indispensable dietary supplement but also as a preservative agent. The large salt playas of Bouara immediately to the east of Qraya (and somewhat to the northeast of Ramadi) offered a significant source of salt, of industrial proportions. It is to be noted that while the Uruk sites in the South had easier access to salt in the marsh areas, such was not the case in the Northern plains where the urban diffusion was taking place. The large settlements at Habuba and Kannas may also have been conditioned, at least in part, by the availability of salt in the nearby Jabbul playas.

Such a suggestion offers itself not only on the basis of geographical considerations, but also and especially as a result of a new assessment of a distinctive Qraya (and more generally Protoliterate) archaeological assemblage. The most typical vessel of this assemblage is the beveled rim bowl. What is most distinctive typologically about these vessels (regular shape, ware including a high degree of porosity, distributional pattern of large amounts found together in thick deposits) happens to be identical to the "briquetage" which in late prehistoric sites in Europe has come to be demonstrably linked with salt production (Hopkinson 1975). The association, at Qraya (and other Protoliterate sites as well) of beveled rim bowls with small ovens/kilns, with large high rim platters (or "trays"), and with ceramic ladles corresponds well with what is known of the manufacturing techniques required for the refinement and consolidation of salt cakes: salt would be first evaporated in the large platters which were resting on the grills inside the ovens, then scooped out into the smaller (beveled rim) bowls and left to dry completely on the edges of the grill. Complete desiccation was necessary because of the high hygroscopic nature of salt. Once so desiccated in the bowls, the salt cakes were probably shipped in the bowls themselves: in spite of the extra weight, the bowls would have insured the better preservation of the salt against moisture; but it is also possible that the salt cakes were placed in lighter containers for shipment. The standardization of the beveled rim bowls, which has been shown to be only approximate (Shimabuku 1976; Beale 1978), would then correspond to the need to have cakes of some generally uniform shape and size for shipment, rather than to the need of exact measurement such as for the distribution of rations.

Whatever the ultimate merit of the "salt hypothesis" for an explanation of the use of the beveled rim bowls, the fact remains that the position of Qraya is so unique as to require some very distinctive interpretive hypothesis. Unlike other Protoliterate sites, Qraya (together with Ramadi) are relatively small *and isolated* settlements, whose nature can hardly be described in terms of either major agricultural centers or way stations on a major overland route. Such a uniqueness of their location, coupled with the presence there of a standard protoliterate assemblage, make for a very intriguing cultural problem which the continuation of our excavations there will hopefully contribute to elucidate.

The issue of the relationship of the Qraya material to the Uruk period material from other sites, and its bearing on chronological distribution, is taken up only briefly in this report, which remains primarily descriptive; it will be discussed more at length in forthcoming, fuller publications of the Qraya material currently planned by Shimabuku and Reimer. As for terminology, we use the term "Protoliterate" to refer to the period as a whole in its historical dimension, and "Uruk (period)" to refer to a particular type of artifact assemblage.

1.3   Publication Program

The series of Qraya reports will follow closely the pattern established by the Joint Expedition to Terqa reports. This includes three major subseries.

The first set consists of *modular* preliminary reports. They deal with relatively narrow segments of the evidence, often conditioned by extrinsic, temporary conditions (typically the duration span of one season of excavations), they reflect a preliminary stage in the evaluation of the evidence and provide a more limited amount of elaboration and documentation. We will use the term "modular" instead of "preliminary" in the series title, because some of the topics covered in these reports will not necessarily be resumed in later reports—as might otherwise be implied by the term "preliminary."

Final reports, on the other hand, include larger groups of data which may be regarded as self-contained from a stratigraphic point of view and comprehensive in terms of data presentation. The main difference from modular reports, then, is that with the final reports (a) no additional information bearing directly on the stratigraphic aspect of the data can be expected from further excavations, while at the same time (b) the scope of the data constitutes a major body of material, presented with full documentary evidence.

The third category of regular publications consists of the *global record,* sorted by period of excavation. This is a computer data base which includes all the data excavated, encoded according to a full categorization system developed especially to take into account the requirements of stratigraphy, and to some extent of typology as well. Encoded in the field directly on the computer, it will provide the most complete and objective record of the data as excavated; this, however, will be possible only for material from future seasons, because for the past ones the encoding was non-digital and not yet fully developed in terms of the current categorization system. (A first sample of this new type of record, together with a revised *Encoding Manual,* is in preparation for the first IIMAS seasons at Mozan.)

The specific titles currently in preparation include the following: Daniel Shimabuku, Report on the 1981 season of excavations; Steven Reimer, Report on the 1984-85 seasons of excavations; Guy Bunnens and Arlette Roobaert-Bunnens, Protoliterate seal impressions. We also have to refer to these publications for a photographic documentation of excavations and finds.

1.4   Acknowledgments

We are pleased to present the first systematic publication of the results of our work at Qraya to the Director General of Antiquities and Museums of Syria, Dr. Afif Behnassi, and to the other officials of the Directorate who have so promptly and generously supported our special endeavors at this site—especially Dr. Adnan Bunni, Director of Excavations, Mr. Kassem Touer, Director of Research, and Mr. As'ad Mahmud, Director of the Museum of Der ez-Zor. Recognizing the urgent need for the safeguard of Qraya, they made it possible for us to undertake our work there as an extension of the main work at Terqa/'Ashara, of which Qraya is in fact a satellite settlement.

The representatives of the Directorate helped us at all times to deal with the sometimes delicate situation arising from the presence of local inhabitants on part of the tell. Over the years, our representatives at Qraya included Messrs. Muhammad Muslim, Khalil Hassani, and Hamido Hammadi: to them goes our sincere appreciation for their role in making our progress there possible.

The local authorities were also very instrumental in helping us to carry out our work and to protect the antiquities of Qraya. We wish to mention here in particular the governors of the province of Der ez-Zor under whose administration the work described in this report took place—Messrs. Abd el-Salam Bitar and Hamid Abu-Hassan. Also, the Chief of Police of Der ez-Zor, Major Muhammad Heikal, has always extended his support in matters pertaining to the protection of the site, as well as the Chiefs of Police of the Mantaqa of Meyadin and the Nahia of Ashara (in whose jurisdiction Qraya lies).

IIMAS — The International Institute for Mesopotamian Area Studies, has been directly responsible for the excavations at Qraya. Funding was made generously available throughout all the seasons by the Ambassador International Cultural Foundation; for the 1983 season Daniel Shimabuku was able to use the research support made available to him by the Fulbright Commission; and in the 1984 and 1985 seasons Steven Reimer obtained partial support from the Institute for Old Testament Related Studies. To these individuals and institutions goes our sincere appreciation for making the Qraya excavations a reality.

Started and carried out under salvage project conditions, the work at Qraya is now yielding evidence of considerable significance for the understanding of the earliest period of human civilization in Syria and the Near East. We trust that our continued cooperative work at the site will yield ever more abundant fruits in the future.

2. The 1977-79 Soundings

by

Kay Simpson

2.1 The Site

Excavations at Qraya were first begun in the fall of 1977. Initial surface inspection by Djobadjet Rouault revealed a mid-second millennium B.C. occupation overlying a larger mid-fourth millennium settlement. Most surface sherds were from the Late Uruk period, but many Ubaid sherds were also observed. The only other evidence of fourth millennium occupation along this stretch of the Middle Euphrates is at Tell ar-Ramadi, north of Tell Hariri (Mari). Tell ar-Ramadi is a small mound, slightly larger than Qraya, with an extensive Late Uruk occupation, no evidence of third millennium settlement, and reoccupation during the first half of the second millennium. This sequence is almost identical to the cultural sequence found at Tell Qraya, save for the lack of Ubaid occupation. Both appear to be small, unwalled, agricultural villages located on excellent bottomland immediately adjacent to the Euphrates.

Tell Qraya lies on the right (west) bank of the Euphrates River 16 km downstream from the Khabūr River junction and 5 km upstream from Tell al 'Ashārah (Fig. 1). As visible above the current plain level, it is a small mound, measuring 130 m north/south by 140 m east/west, and is roughly oval in shape (Fig. 2).

The site sits on top of a natural gravel promontory. This gravel bank, a rare formation along this stretch of the Middle Euphrates, has protected the main portion of the site from the severe erosive action the river has inflicted on nearby Tell 'Ashārah and Tell Mayādīn. The promontory forms a small spur created by an ancient meander loop north of the mound.

A pumphouse on the north side of the mound feeds a major east/west canal system. This pumphouse rests on a small gravel fan flattened by erosion. Little cultural material has been found on the fan and it appears not to have been part of the original mound. The plain west of Qraya supports productive cotton fields and valuable groves of poplar trees. An area formed by a remnant channel of the Euphrates lies 2 m lower than the surrounding plain and is criss-crossed by many small agricultural plots. The high land south of Qraya is dotted with hamlets linking the older houses on Tell Qraya with the newer village (Baladiyah) of Qraya 1 km south. They are all part of the Nahya of 'Asharah.

Seventeen major modern house compounds cover the mound, mostly on its western side. Most older houses are of adobe construction. The installation of new concrete block houses has damaged portions of the south side of the site. Around 1976 the villagers of Qraya bulldozed upper levels on the southern and eastern sides of the mound, obliterating natural contours, and creating two stepped flat areas for future construction and agricultural projects. These upper levels, mostly second millennium strata, were pushed over the side of the mound into the Euphrates. Intact second millennium strata still exist beneath house compounds clustered on the west side of the mound, but these are badly disturbed. On the northeast side a utility pole was embedded in a detached column over 2 m high with stratified mid-second millennium deposits. This column stood as a dismal testament to the original height of the east side of the settlement and even it was recently removed by the villagers. At the base of this pillar the survey team found courses of mud brick and vessels similar to forms recovered from second millennium levels at Terqa.

The Joint Expedition to Terqa requested that bulldozing and other leveling activities be suspended on the site. Tell Qraya is now registered with the Department of Antiquities and is subject to protective measures under Syrian law.

This site report underscores two problems of archaeological context present on most sites I have surveyed in the Middle Euphrates area (Simpson 1983). One is the extensive destruction occurring on small mounds in the valley. Cultural impacts from modern construction are altering the configuration of mounds in this area to a degree unmatched throughout antiquity. Although the erosive force of the Euphrates River undoubtedly has removed sites when it cuts new channels, and the river is now severely eroding several right bank sites in the survey area, human land modification projects aided by modern land leveling machines are far more destructive. The other is the problem of assessing site occupation by surface collection. Initial assessments of the site from surface sherds accurately accounted for the extensive Late Uruk occupation, but overestimated Ubaid occupation. The extent of second millennium occupation will probably never be accurately assessed. Land modification projects have irretrievably altered the configuration and depth of deposits at this mound.

2.2 History of Excavations

Because almost three-fifths of the mound lies under modern housing and the open areas are covered with several meters of modern debris and backdirt from the bulldozer operations, systematic surface collecting of artifacts was not done. Backdirt also hampered inspection of stratigraphy exposed along the high northern and eastern slopes before the dropoff into the Euphrates. The following squares (abbreviated SG) and features (FT) have been excavated in the three seasons of work at the site.

SG 1. The survey team had observed courses of mud brick exposed along the bulldozer cut on the southeastern side of the mound, 40 m west of the dropoff into the river. In November 1977 Olivier Rouault and William Shelby cleaned a section face (designated SG 1) 6.30 m in length along this slope cut and exposed mud brick walls at the north end (FT 1) and at the south end (FT 2). The section was divided into four loci; three loci were 2 m lengthwise and one locus, north of FT 1, was 0.3 m long (Fig. 3). At least seven courses of brick could be discerned in FT 1 and three courses in FT 2. In between the two sections of wall the soil consisted of a series of eroded bricky fills. Soft ashy soil on the north side of FT 1 and the south side of FT 2 indicated room fill.

The section face was cut back 20 cm, and artifacts were collected in 30 cm deep arbitrary levels. Four levels were excavated down to the base of the bulldozer cut. The section yielded Uruk period pottery, including a large number of beveled rim bowl sherds, and chert and obsidian flakes and blades. A complete beveled rim bowl was found in the room fill south of FT 2. The soft fill of the upper strata of SG 1 contained few second millennium ceramics, though a few sherds of a thin-walled, highly fired ware similar to one found at Terqa were recovered.

SG 2. After ascertaining that at least a meter of Uruk period depositional strata were intact in Locus 4, Rouault and Shelby laid a 4 m × 4 m square south of Locus 4 to explore room fill associated with FT 2. The square was initially divided into four 1 m × 1 m loci. Preliminary cleaning revealed a crosswall to FT 2, and loci were redefined to reflect areas inside and outside the room (Fig. 4a). The 1977 team excavated two 30 cm deep arbitrary levels in the area west of the room (Loci 1 and 2), one level inside the room (Locus 8), and then trenched the room in a 1 m × 2 m locus (Locus 13) adjacent to the north wall (FT 2). They also excavated one level north of FT 2 (Locus 15).

While a major effort had been planned for the 1978 field season, excavations at Qraya had to be sacrificed on account of the Municipal Project salvage excavations at Terqa that season. Excavation commenced under my direction in SG 2, Locus 13, but was quickly terminated (Buccellati 1979:16).

On November 19, 1979, I resumed excavations at Qraya. I reopened SG 2 and excavated the east half of the square (the area enclosed by the two crosswalls) down to sterile by natural excavation units. As the baulks were now heavily eroded, the square was readjusted slightly to make a 3 m × 3 m locus (Locus 17) inclusive of the lower strata of Locus 13 (Fig. 4b).

SG 3 and SG 4. In the 1979 season a long 15 m × 1.5 m step trench (SG 3) was placed on the far northeast side of the mound. Here elevations dropped 6 m within 15 m along the slope before a steep dropoff into the river. Extensive backdirt covered the lower slope but was light along the upper slope. It was hoped the trench would uncover intact second millennium strata on the upper slope as Old Babylonian period sherds had been found in this vicinity. Unfortunately, excavations soon revealed an enormous borrow pit 10 m wide and at least 2 m deep had destroyed deposits from the lower slope.

However, a badly eroded wall associated with mixed second and fourth millennium ceramics was present on the upper slope west of the borrow pit. A second step trench (SG 4) was placed adjacent to SG 3, but pivoted away from the borrow pit. This trench dropped 4 m in elevation within 12.5 m along the slope before terminating at the river dropoff. Five loci were declared. Modern debris was removed and the upper stratum in each locus was excavated. The tops of two walls were exposed, but ceramics from all strata continued to be mixed second and fourth millennium wares.

2.3 Description of Strata in SG 2

In SG 2 the following strata and features were recorded. Stratigraphic terms follow the system outlined in Buccellati and Kelly-Buccellati (1978). Rouault and Shelby excavated strata 0-8 in 1977 (The QR1 excavation season), and I excavated strata 9-15 in 1978 (QR2) and 1979 (QR3) (Figs. 5-6).

Stratum 0. Almost 2 m of soft bulldozer backfill and garbage covered the fourth millennium deposits. A thin shell of hardened soil capped the ancient deposit.

Stratum 1. In the southwest corner of Locus 1 a thick, soft fill deposit of bricky material overlies a section of brick wall (FT 1). In FT 1 three courses of mud brick stood on end. A clay lens, 1-2 cm thick, below the second brick course may have been a floor surface. Because FT 1 was in the far southwest corner it was only partially excavated.

Stratum 2. Stratum 1 cut into this hard-packed, bricky fill. This fill was deposited after the collapse of the highest standing section of a mud brick wall in Stratum 3.

Stratum 3. Below the hard-packed fill three lenses of fine-grained, clayey-silt sloped away from mud brick rubble (FT A) and sections of two mud brick walls (FT B-C). The lowest lens consisted of a fine-grained, light-colored clay on top of a black sooted floor flush with the top of FT B.

Stratum 4. On the northwest side of FT A-C in Locus 2 five clay lenses sloped away from the wall and associated rubble. These layers did not appear to be floors but fine-grained deposition that slowly filled a depression.

Stratum 5. Underneath the last floor of Stratum 3 was another soft, bricky fill deposit. The lower levels of Stratum 3 and Stratum 5 were cut by an inclusion of bright-red burned soil.

Stratum 6. Below Stratum 5 was another fill layer of bricky material that included burnt brickbats and plaster fragments.

Stratum 7. Underneath the rubble on the north side of FT A-B was a thin layer of deposition that may have been a floor associated with FT B. This deposit was exposed in only a small area of the square.

Stratum 8. FT 4 designated three basin-shaped ovens made of scorched and hardened mud. They are west of the north-south crosswall (FT 3) of ST 1. An indistinct floor surface (FT 6) linked FT 4 to the base of FT 3. These basins are similar in shape to basins found in domestic structures at Habuba Kabira South (Sürenhagen 1978:Karte 4).

Stratum 9. Structure 1 consisted of a small room with three low walls (FT 2, 3, and 21) preserved. The missing east wall was probably clipped off by the bulldozer, as was most of the south wall (FT 21) and part of the north wall (FT 2). The tiny stub of the south wall (FT 21), one course deep, was exposed only in section. Another wall stub was attached to the northwest side of FT 3 and is associated with another structure. The extant room width of ST 1 was 3 m north-south, but length of the room cannot be calculated. Most domestic structures at Habuba Kabira South were 3 m × 2 m (Bunnens 1982). In the 1977 excavation of Locus 8 an irregular floor (FT 5) embedded with pebbles, sherds, bone, and charcoal was described in association with FT 3.

Stratum 10. The walls of ST 1 were set into a loose, ashy fill packed with sherds and bone. Several whole beveled rim bowls were found in this fill. The upper fill consisted of two major lenses of ash and charcoal (FT 19). Beneath these lenses was a soft, reddish-brown silt lens (FT 22), and below FT 22 was a light gray ashy matrix composed of three major lenses (FT 23). These lenses tilted eastward across the square, and were thinnest next to FT 2. They did not extend to the east baulk, but had been removed by the bulldozer cut.

Stratum 11. In the southwest corner of the locus were the remains of a fire pit or oven (FT 24), more substantial than the basin structures of FT 4 in Locus 1 and 2. Several large sherds were embedded in hard-packed, ash-streaked, red soil surrounded by bright red fired brick fragments. This oven was covered by FT 25, a thick fill of hard, compacted reddish-brown bricky debris, the top of which had been intentionally leveled. Underneath FT 24 and 25 was FT 26, a light gray-brown matrix with black ash deposits, such as FT 8. A burned beam fragment from this debris provided a C-14 sample. At the interface of FT 25 and FT 26 were several whole objects. A large storage vessel, a cluster of grinding stones, and a down-turned beveled rim bowl were on the floor of FT 26. Very few sherds or other artifactual debris were present.

Stratum 12. The above layers of burned and bricky debris rested on a series of bright yellow-brown laminated floors 10-12 cm thick (FT 9). Six major floors were counted. The lowest floor appeared as a dark brown stain in section. The upper floors had been evenly leveled off. Floors were very clean with only a few tiny river pebbles and artifacts present. Underneath FT 9 was a level greenish-gray floor ca. 4 cm thick (FT 10), and underneath that floor was a bright pink floor ca. 1 cm thick (FT 11A) which extended across the entire locus.

Stratum 13. Under this series of leveled floors were the abbreviated remains of ST 2. Its two crosswalls (FT 12 and 13) were almost identical in orientation to the west and north walls of ST 1. These walls were composed of tuff-like mud packing, not regular brick coursing. Wall faces were eroded and difficult to define. FT 13 had been leveled off to an even 44-45 cm from base to top, prior to use-life of the floors in Stratum 12. Both walls rested on a foundation of fine river sand (FT 27). Feature 27 had a pronounced dip westward. This sand foundation was laid on top of a leveled surface, but the mud brick pack was laid more irregularly on top of the sand.

Within the room was a compacted, gray-green, lumpy fill (FT 15—not shown in section) leveled off flush with the top of the walls. An artifact concentration of beveled rim bowls and other broken vessels, blade and flake tools, and ground stone implements (FT 11B) lay near the wall corner and along FT 12. A concentration of animal bone (Bone Lot 2553) was jammed into the north wall near the northwest wall corner.

Two adult and one juvenile sheep were found in this bone lot. Horn cores indicate that one adult was a male. Few ribs or vertebrae were present, but many pieces of the lower limb, cranial-mandible fragments, and a complete dentition were there. This composition of bone types is very typical of room floor deposits. The association of lower limb and cranial fragments suggest a butchering practice (still the norm in Syria) of removing the head and feet in one location and finishing the butchering elsewhere. Also present in this lot were fragments of an infant and an adult goat.

Stratum 14. Underneath the walls and room fill was a thick, hard-packed yellow-brown bricky fill (FT 16). A lens of tiny river pebbles marked its upper layer. Most artifacts collected from this stratum were from the pebble lens, including a reddish buff, thin-ware vessel with a pouring lip which appears to be earlier than Late Uruk. FT 29 (not shown in section) was a pocket of pebbles under FT 12. Few artifacts were retrieved from the lower fill, but many brickbats were present. It could not be ascertained if this feature was intentional fill or compaction of a previous wall. A small, 20 cm X 20 cm clay bin (FT 28, not shown in section) lay near the surface of FT 16. In the northwest corner of the locus, underneath the wall corner, an irregular pit or borrow area (FT 17) had been cut. It consisted of charcoal flecked with striations of sand, clay, and ash lenses. Pebbles formed the bottom lens. This soil may have been imported fill used to level off an irregularity in FT 16 before the walls of ST 2 (FT 12 and 13) were laid.

Stratum 15. The earliest cultural material consisted of a mottled black ashy matrix with many plaster fragments (FT 18). A thick lens of green slag ran through the far west side of the locus. Lithics, especially obsidian blades, and splinters of animal bone, unfortunately all unidentifiable, were found in abundance. Large slag lots were collected, but few sherds were present. The few sherds found were all small body sherds of an unidentified friable, fugitive-red painted ware.

Sterile soil (FT 30) consisted of extremely hard, reddish-brown clay liberally mixed with pebbles and small stones. Some cultural material occurred near the old land surface, mostly small, fragmentary pieces of animal bone, lithics, and flecks of ash.

2.4 Summary and Interpretation of the Features

Three building phases and 13 associated floors were present in 3 m of Late Uruk period deposits in SG 2. Little can be said concerning the upper phase of which only two badly disturbed wall sections remain (FT A-C, FT 1). The middle phase (ST 1) is probably part of a domestic building complex. The three basin-shaped ovens (FT 4) in SG 2 Locus 1 and the tiny wall stub in Locus 2 are associated with another room west of Structure 1. Structure 1 may be contemporary with SG 1 FT 1 and its associated room fill to the north of the wall. Structure 1 was identically aligned with the lowest building phase (ST 2). Structure 2 was leveled intentionally prior to installation of ST 1. Structure 1 also may have been leveled after its use life.

There is little architectural or artifactual evidence for specialized activities. Room fill and floor debris are entirely domestic in character.

2.5 Ceramics (by William R. Shelby and Kay Simpson)

Ceramic material from the sounding has been rough sorted by form and design into provisional types and wares. Sherds were counted by ware type for 50 percent of the pottery lots from Locus 17. Table 1 shows ware counts by stratum. A comprehensive ceramic analysis has not been made yet, but this typology of 904 sherds clearly indicates a homogeneous corpus of Late Uruk forms and wares with a small admixture of two Ubaid wares.

The IIMAS typological sequence for form analysis classes vessels by size, shape, decoration, and ware (Buccellati and Kelly-Buccellati 1978:22-23; Kelly-Buccellati and Shelby 1977: 182-183). The small size of the ceramic corpus precluded fine distinctions in size graduations among vessel types. The general shapes in the Qraya corpus include bowls (Figs. 7, 8, and 13a), jars (Figs. 9-11 and 13b), spouts (Fig. 12), and plates (Fig. 13c).

Table 1. Distribution of Uruk and Ubaid period ware types by strata, Locus 17, SG2.

STRATA	Red Ware	Gray Ware	Reserve Slip Ware	Coarse Ware	Coarse Combed Ware	Plant Tempered Coarse Ware	Wet Smoothed Ware	Wiped Ware	Fine Ware	Beveled Rim Bowl Ware	Unidentified Buff Ware	Unidentified Fugitive Red Ware	Dark Brown Painted Ware	Green Plainware	TOTAL
9	-	-	-	--	--	--	--		1	---	---	-	-	-	1
10	5	-	-	11	24	2	24	11	7	253	36	-	-	-	373
11	1	1	7	26	20	3	9	66	7	144	35	-	6	-	325
12	-	-	-	--	--	--	--	--	--	---	---	-	-	-	---
13	1	1	1	3	9	--	1	13	7	71	23	-	1	4	135
14	1	-	-	14	2	13	13	--	--	7	20	-	-	1	71
15	-	-	-	--	--	--	--	--	--	---	---	present*	-	-	---
TOTAL	8	2	8	54	55	18	47	90	21	475	114		7	5	904

*not counted

Internal division of Early, Middle, and Late Uruk are primarily based on stratigraphic and architectural divisions at a few key sites, not on ceramic seriation. Seriations such as Johnson's (1973:31-45) analysis of the ceramic material from the Susa Acropole sounding indicate that development from Middle to Late Uruk is characterized more by proportional changes in ceramic types than by replacement of old types by new types.

Straight spouts, impressed strip bowls, and red and gray wares may indicate an Early-Middle Uruk component at Qraya, but the site lacks truly characteristic Early Uruk types such as pointed base bottles and net-like painting. The association of such distinctive shapes as beveled rim bowls, strap handles, drooping spouts, and husking trays, in conjunction with a variety of surface finishes such as incising, impressed strips, and reserved slip points to a Late Uruk occupation. Many Late Uruk types and wares found at this site continue into the Jamdat Nasr and Early Dynastic I periods. A wet smoothed ware (Ware TM) and a reserved slip ware, but with horizontal and not oblique lines (Ware TK), are found in early third millennium contexts at Terqa (Buccellati 1979:72-75). However, diagnostic Jamdat Nasr painted wares and conical cups are absent.

The following Uruk period wares have been identified at Qraya.

Red Ware. This ware is always painted bright red, sometimes with discernible burnish marks almost approaching a polish. It was fired at a medium low temperature; a light streak may show in section. Temper is mineral, usually sand, small pebbles, or mica. There are occasional inclusions of plant temper. Often sand is visible through the red paint on the exterior. Hardness averages 2 on the Moh's scale. Red ware appeared in low frequencies throughout the upper strata of SG 2 and in the lower strata (Table 1).

A variety of vessel forms occur in this ware at Qraya, such as inverted rim bowls (Fig. 8j), flat rim bowls (Fig. 8i), straight spouted vessels (Fig. 12c), and four lugged jars. The flat rim bowls are similar in form to vessels dated to the Susa A period (Le Breton 1957:93) and to surface material from the Susiana survey (Johnson 1973:Table 3). Straight spouts are considered highly diagnostic for Early Uruk by Johnson (1973:55), Lloyd (1948:48), and Adams and Nissen (1972:100). Red ware occurs in Middle-Late Uruk levels XIII-IV (concentrated in VI) at Warka, and in Middle-transitional-to-Late Uruk levels XX-XVI (concentrated in XIX) at Nippur (Hansen 1965:292). However, Qraya red ware is painted, not slipped or burnished as found at Warka. At Nineveh, red ware is associated with the later levels (Lloyd 1948:44-46), and it is found at Grai Resh in unstratified contexts (Lloyd 1938:140). Four-lugged red ware jars appear in Inanna XIX (Middle Uruk). Thus red ware cannot be considered diagnostic of either the Middle or Late Uruk phases.

Gray Ware. Gray ware vessels are burnished with a very smooth exterior though interiors are left rough. The ware is tempered with sand and occasionally with small pebbles. It is fired at medium temperature and shatters with fracture planes parallel to the surface of the vessel. Only a few body sherds of gray ware have been found at Qraya, not enough to identify vessel types.

Gray ware is present in Early Uruk levels at Warka and Eridu (Lloyd 1948:46). Gray burnished ware also occurs in Grai Resh IV-II, Nineveh III, and Gaura XI-Xa; all "Gaura" period levels encompass the entire Uruk period (Perkins 1949:Table 3).

Reserve Slip Ware. This ware has a buff-yellow slip applied over a darker clay. It is usually diagonally slipped (Fig. 10c). The ware is tempered with finely chopped organic material, and may have sand and small pebbles as inclusions. In sherds from larger vessels the temper particles are quite large. The ware is generally high fired. Hardness on Moh's scale is 2.

Reserve slip ware has a wide chronological distribution within the Uruk period. It is found in Middle Uruk-Early Dynastic I levels at Nippur (Hansen 1965:292-293), Early-Middle Uruk levels at Tell-i-Chazir (Dyson 1965:224), and in Late Uruk levels at Susa (Le Breton 1957: 100). Delougaz (1952:53, Plate 39) gives examples of ED I reserved slip jars from Khafjah. Adams (1965:127) used reserved slip ware as a diagnostic Protoliterate c-d (Jamdat Nasr) and ED I ware type in his Diyala survey. In the vicinity of the site of Warka, Adams and Nissen (1972) found the ware on both Early and Late Uruk sites but considered the ware highly diagnostic of ED I sites.

Coarse Ware. This plainware is orange-buff in color. Its paste often has large lumps of clean clay embedded in it, with large pebbles and micas as temper. Organic temper is rare. Carbon streaks are common in section. Hardness on the Moh's scale is 3. Round rim bowls, common in this ware, have a wide chronological distribution. They occur in Early Uruk contexts in the Susiana plain (Johnson 1973:54), in Late Uruk contexts at Susa (Le Breton 1957), and throughout the Uruk sequence at Tepe Farukhabad (Wright 1969).

Course Combed Ware. This ware is similar to Coarse Ware but has combing on the exterior, usually only on the upper body (Fig. 9a). Combed patterns are done either in parallel lines or irregularly crisscrossed lines. Exterior applied designs occur. Color ranges from red to buff. Temper is sand with large organic particles, pebbles, and mica as minor components. Vessel interiors are usually wiped. Moh's scale ranges from 3 to 4.

Impressed strip bowls and jars (Fig. 11b) occur in this ware at Qraya. Impressed strip bowls have been found in the Early Uruk levels (Levels 24-21) at the Susa Acropole sounding (Johnson 1973:Table 6) and at Warka Levels XIII-XII (Noldeke et al. 1932; Johnson 1973:Table 11). Impressed strip jar shoulders were defined as a transitional Middle-Late type in the Susiana surface collections (Johnson 1973:56) and as a hallmark for the Late Uruk in the Warka regional survey collections (Nissen 1972:100). Surface combing is found in both Middle and Late Uruk contexts at Nippur (Hansen 1965).

Plant-Tempered Coarse Ware. This ware, another plainware variant, contains large amounts of organic "chaff temper." Occasionally small pebbles are mixed in the paste. Tempering material is quite visible on the exterior. Carbon streaks are common in the thicker examples. Color ranges from orange-buff to orange. Moh's scale is 2.

Sherds of chaff-tempered trays (Fig. 8L) were found. These are thick-rimmed vessels with large amounts of organic material and small pebbles in the paste. Such trays are present in Middle and Late Uruk levels at Warka and Nippur, and in the later levels at Susa (Johnson 1973). These vessels have been intepreted as husking trays (Nissen 1972:100).

Wiped Ware. This buff to red-orange ware is wiped on the exterior and sometimes on its interior as well. It is organic tempered with small stones as inclusions. Sherds can have coarse, pit-marked exteriors; but most often exteriors are smoothed. Firing is medium. Vessel forms have not been identified at Qraya for this ware but a number of body sherds occurred in strata 10, 11, 13.

Thin-Walled Fine Ware. Vessels of this ware are buff to orange in color. Fine sand was used as a tempering agent. These vessels occasionally were decorated with incised parallel lines on the exterior, and some sherds have been scraped on the exterior. Moh's scale is 3. Small jars with carinated bodies and flaring rims and small deep bowls (Fig. 9a) have been found at Qraya.

Beveled Rim Bowl Ware. This bowl, the hallmark of the Late Uruk period, is recognized by its obliquely cut rim. It has the dubious distinction of being one of the homeliest pottery types found in ancient Western Asia. The ware is extremely porous, poorly fired, and made of clay heavily tempered with organic material with sand and small pebbles as inclusions. Some mica is found in the Qraya examples. Color ranges from buff to orange but is usually a distinctive yellow. Carbon streaks are common in thicker examples. Finger impressions are often found on interiors and mold(?) impressions of sand and earth on exteriors. It is thought to be mold-made and to have been manufactured in large quantities (Nissen 1972:99; Sürenhagen 1978). Recently Kalsbeek (1980) has demonstrated an alternate manufacturing technique. Few finishing techniques are applied to the surface.

Many complete beveled rim bowls (Fig. 7a, b) were recovered from the sounding, as well as several thousand sherds, including many that were rim-to-base. Sherds were found in all strata except the lowest, Stratum 15, in SG 2. Beveled rim bowl sherds accounted for over 50 percent of all counted sherds in Strata 9-14 (Table 1).

Two Ubaid ware types have been identified at Qraya. Though often found in surface collection on the site Ubaid sherds occur in low frequencies in excavated strata of SG 2 (Table 1). As strata with only Ubaid sherds were not found in the SG 2 sounding, the Ubaid settlement was probably smaller than the Late Uruk component and is located under a different section of the mound.

Dark Brown Painted Ware. This ware has designs painted in brown over a light buff background. Occasionally the designs are painted on a greenish or red background. Vessels are tempered with very fine sand. In the thicker shapes a light streak is found in section. Thinner shapes appear to be fired at high temperatures while thicker shapes were fired at lower temperatures. Most sherds of this ware recovered in the sounding are small body sherds, but shallow bowls (Fig. 13a), jar handles (Fig. 13b), and portions of ladder pattern designs have been found.

Green Plainware. This buff ware appears to the eye to have a light "greenish" cast. It is tempered with fine sand, with some small pebbles and organic material as inclusions. Sherds from thin-walled plates have been found in this ware (Fig. 13c). Since there were very few of these sherds found, it is possible that this is a ware of the Uruk period.

Second Millennium Wares. Sherds from the early-to-mid-second millennium B.C. are scattered over the surface of the mound, but have been found *in situ* only on the high remnants

Table 2. Minimum number of individuals by species:
SG2, Tell Qraya.

Stratum/ Feature	Ovis aries	Capra hircus	Bos taurus	Equus asinus	Capreolus capreolus	Canis	Aves	Pisces	Total
ST 10; FT 19	2	1	-	-	-	-	P	-	3
ST 10; FT 22	2	-	-	1	-	1	-	-	4
ST 11; FT 24	2	1	1	-	1	-	P	-	5
ST 11; FT 25	1	2	-	-	-	-	-	-	3
ST 12; FT 10	1	1	-	-	-	-	P	-	2
ST 13; FT 11	3	1	-	-	-	-	-	-	4
ST 13; FT 15	2	2	-	-	-	-	-	-	4
ST 14; FT 17	1	3	-	-	-	-	P	-	4
ST 14; FT 16	1	2	1	1	1	-	-	-	6
ST 15; FT 18	1	2	-	-	1	-	-	-	4
TOTAL	16	15	2	2	3	1	P	-	39

P = Present, but uncounted.

of the upper portion of the site. Most sherds were found in the erosional debris at the base of the mound and in bulldozer backfill. Button-based vessels, ovoid jars (Fig. 14a), and platters (Fig. 14b) similar to those found in levels at Tell al 'Ashārah dated to the second quarter of the second millennium B.C. were found stratified in the telephone column which was left standing while the rest of the second millennium strata were bulldozed away in this area. Sherds similar to Ware D, a fine-tempered plainware found at Tell al 'Ashārah, were the most common second millennium ware type observed.

2.6 Lithics

All strata contained an abundance of flint and obsidian blades. Debitage and cores occurred less frequently. Many flint blades glistened with "sickle sheen." Ground stone objects were common, especially on floor surfaces. Lithic artifacts will be analyzed at a later date.

2.7 Faunal Remains (by Kathleen F. Galvin)

Osteological material from the 1978 and 1979 (QR2-3) seasons were analyzed in conjunction with material from second and third millennia deposits from the site of Tell al 'Ashārah. Methods of analysis are discussed in Galvin (1981). Bone from levels in SG 2 (Table 2) and SG 4 (Table 3) were analyzed.

Techniques of recovery affected the number of bones recovered as well as the diversity of species identifiable in the collection. Some levels, especially from SG 4, were removed with small and large picks. This increased the fragmentation of already moist, friable bone. The lack of fine screening in some levels reduced the quantity of small bones recovered. Therefore, the sample of bone recovered from the test excavations gives only a very general picture of the relative abundance of domestic and wild fauna at Qraya.

In the collection of 2,373 bone fragments (6.78 kgs) only 188 (8 percent) were identifiable to the Family or a finer level of classification. The 188 identifiable bones resulted in species identifications which could be interpreted as a minimum number of individuals (MNI) of 48. Birds and fish were not included in this MNI, but were recorded on the basis of presence or absence only.

Forty-three percent of the total MNI were identified as *Ovis aries* (Table 4) and 37 percent as *Capra hircus* (Table 5). All bone identified as *Ovis* and *Capra* exhibited the morphological characteristics and range of variation in size expected for domestic species, and show no significant differences from the bones of domestic sheep and goat recovered from second millennium B.C. and Medieval strata at Tell al 'Ashārah. This faunal evidence suggests that little morphological change has taken place in sheep and goat populations since the fourth millennium B.C.

Age category percentages differ markedly for the two populations (Table 6). The largest percentage of deaths for *Ovis aries* occurred in the Adult category (60 percent), with deaths in the Infant and Juvenile categories equally divided at 20 percent each. As argued in my analysis of the Tell al 'Ashārah bone material (Galvin 1981), the high percentage of individuals in the Adult category may reflect an emphasis in the economy on the use of herds for wool. Meat

Table 3. Minimum number of individuals by species:
SG4, Tell Qraya.

Stratum/ Feature	Ovis aries	Capra hircus	Bos taurus	Equus asinus	Capreolus capreolus	Canis	Aves	Pisces	Total
ST 1; FT 2, 3	2	1	-	-	-	-	P	-	3
ST 1; FT 5, 6	-	-	1	-	-	1	P	P	2
ST 1; FT 8,9,10	2	1	2	-	-	-	P	-	5
TOTAL	4	2	3	-	-	1	P	P	10

P = Present, but uncounted.

Table 4. Remains of sheep (*Ovis aries*), Tell Qraya.

EXCAVATION UNIT	SG 2			SG 4, FT 1				
	ST 13	ST 17	ST 18-20	FT 2, 3	FT 5, 6	FT 8-10	FT 12	TOTAL
Other	2	2						4
Phalanx 3				1				1
Phalanx 2								-
Phalanx 1		3	1					4
Metapodial		1				1		2
Astragalus	1	1						2
Calcaneum	1							1
Tibia								-
Femur	1	1	1					3
Pelvis								-
Ulna						1		1
Radius	1	1				1		3
Humerus		1						1
Scapula	1	1				1		3
Axis								-
Mandible	4	8						12
Maxilla	1	6		2		2		11
Skull Fragment		1						1
Horn Core	1					1		2
Minimal Number Individuals	5	8	3	2	-	2	-	20
Number Fragments Identified	13	25	3	3	-	7	-	51

Table 5. Remains of goat (*Capra hircus*), Tell Qraya.

EXCAVATION UNIT	SG 2			SG 4, ST 1				
	ST 13	ST 17	ST 18-20	FT 2, 3	FT 5, 6	FT 8-10	FT 12	TOTAL
Other		1	1					2
Phalanx 3	1							4
Phalanx 2		1		2				3
Phalanx 1	2	3						5
Metapodial		1	1					2
Astragalus	1	2						3
Calcaneum								-
Tibia								-
Femur			2					2
Pelvis								-
Ulna								-
Radius	1							1
Humerus	1							1
Scapula								-
Axis								-
Mandible	2	6	4			1		13
Maxilla	3	3	3			1		10
Skull Fragment	1							1
Horn Core				1				1
Minimal Number Individuals	5	4	6	1	1			17
Number Fragments Identified	12	16	11	5		2		46

Table 6. Age breakdown by species, Tell Qraya.

SPECIES	AGE CATEGORY			TOTAL
	Infant	Juvenile	Adult	
Ovis aries	4 (.20)	12 (.60)	4 (.20)	20
Capra hircus	2 (.12)	7 (.41)	8 (.47)	17
Bos taurus	-	-	1	1
Equus asinus	-	-	1	1
Capreolus capreolus	-	1 (.33)	2 (.67)	3

Table 7. Remains of cattle (*Bos taurus*), Tell Qraya.

EXCAVATION UNIT	STRATUM/FEATURE	Number Fragments Identified	Minimal Number Individuals	Horn Core	Skull Fragment	Maxilla	Mandible	Atlas	Axis	Scapula	Humerus	Radius	Ulna	Pelvis	Femur	Tibia	Calcaneum	Astragalus	Metapodial	Phalanx 1	Phalanx 2	Phalanx 3	Other
SG 2	ST 13	1	1	-	-	-	1	-	-	-	-	-	-	-	-	-	-	-	-	-	-	-	-
	ST 17	4	1	-	-	-	-	-	-	-	-	-	-	-	-	-	1	-	-	1	1	1	-
	ST 18, 19, 20	-	-	-	-	-	-	-	-	-	-	-	-	-	-	-	-	-	-	-	-	-	-
Total		5	2	-	-	-	1	-	-	-	-	-	-	-	-	-	1	-	-	1	1	1	-
SG 4	ST 1 FT 2, 3	-	-	-	-	-	-	-	-	-	-	-	-	-	-	-	-	-	-	-	-	-	-
	ST 1 FT 5, 6	1	1	-	-	-	1	-	-	-	-	-	-	-	-	-	-	-	-	-	-	-	-
	ST 1 FT 8-10	2	2	-	-	-	-	-	-	-	1	-	-	-	-	-	-	-	-	-	1	-	-
	ST 1 FT 12	-	-	-	-	-	-	-	-	-	-	-	-	-	-	-	-	-	-	-	-	-	-
Total		3	3	-	-	-	1	-	-	-	1	-	-	-	-	-	-	-	-	-	1	-	-
GRAND TOTAL SG 2 & SG 4		8	5	-	-	-	2	-	-	-	1	-	-	-	-	-	1	-	-	1	2	1	-

was not harvested at an age at which both quantity and quality would be optimal, but at a later age.

In contrast, *Capra hircus* shows only 12 percent in the Infant category, 41 percent in the Juvenile, and 47 percent in the Adult categories. The higher frequency of deaths in the Juvenile category compared to *Ovis aries* may indicate the use of goats as a source of prime meat. However, as the highest percentage of deaths still falls in the Adult category other products, such as dairy goods or lower grade meat, may have been important economic considerations.

Only five individuals of *Bos* were identified (10 percent of the total MNI, Table 7). All remains fall within the range of the domestic *Bos taurus* though the lack of any horn cores prevents identification of cattle at the subspecific level. By comparison with sheep and goat, cattle represented a much smaller part of the domestic fauna at this site. This pattern was repeated at nearby Tell al 'Ashārah in all periods.

A small domestic dog within the size range of a modern fox terrier is represented by four canid bones. Three individuals of the roe deer *Capreolus capreolus* were identified on the basis of dentition and postcranial bone. No horn cores were recovered. Only one individual could be identified as *Equus*. This identification was based on characteristics of two third premolars and a second molar. Dentition correspond most closely to the domestic donkey *Equus asinus*.

Bird species identified include *Anser* (goose), *Columba* (dove), and a wading bird of the Order Ciconiiformes. The only fish species identified is a catfish of the Order Cypriniformes.

The faunal material recovered at Tell Qraya indicates that sheep and goat dominate the domestic fauna with a much smaller percentage of cattle present. This pattern is remarkably similar to the pattern found in the faunal assemblage recovered from second millennium B.C. Terqa. The high percentages of individuals in the Adult category for all three species indicates that herds were not raised strictly for the production of prime meat, but for other products best harvested from an adult animal.

The remains of wild fauna are significantly less common than those of domesticates. In comparison with the faunal remains from the second millennium B.C. deposits at Tell al 'Ashārah, wild fauna remains are much richer at Tell Qraya. This was especially true for water fowl. Deer represented 6 percent of the total MNI at the Qraya sounding, but only 2 percent of a much larger sample at Tell al 'Ashārah. Hopefully, larger exposures at Qraya and Tell al 'Ashārah will produce a sample large enough to see if this decline if wild fauna is born out.

2.8 Other Material. No seals, seal impressions, or other types of epigraphic material have been found either from the soundings or from surface inspection. Nor were clay nails or cones for architectural mosaics found. Musil (1927:198) reported that cuneiform tablets had been found at "Tall el-Krejje," which may be Qraya, but the Syrian Department of Antiquities has no confirmed reports from the site.

2.9 Summary

Tell Qraya was initially settled some time during the Ubaid, occupied extensively in the Late Uruk period, abandoned near the beginning of the third millennium, and then reoccupied a millennium later in the Old Babylonian period.

No architectural evidence or artifactual material (e.g., cone mosaics) indicate the presence of anything other than domestic structures at the site. A subsistence economy relying on sheep and goat which may have been augmented with wild game seems indicated. The occupants in the Late Uruk period were engaged in long distance trade for obsidian. No kilns, wasters, or dumps indicate onsite ceramic production, but few of these features have been found in Mesopotamian sites.

The Qraya ceramics have strong typological parallels to forms and designs found at Warka 650 km to the south and Habuba Kabira South 250 km to the north. The material culture of Habuba Kabira and surrounding sites on the Great Bend of the Middle Euphrates is dissimilar to materials from contemporary sites in western Syria and northern Iraq. Therefore, it has been plausibly suggested that these settlements are colonies founded from southern Mesopotamia to control trade routes or, less plausibly, to directly administer this area.

The two Late Uruk period sites in the vicinity of Terqa, Tell Qraya and Tell ar-Ramadī, provide a geographic link between the southern Mesopotamian plain and the Uruk enclaves in the Great Bend area. The presence of these two Uruk settlements within 50 km of each other separated by a gap of 500 km from the nearest known Uruk settlement in the south (no Uruk sites are reported in the Haditha Dam area) suggests a line of widely spaces settlements from southern Mesopotamia up the Euphrates. No longer can the Great Bend sites be considered isolated outposts; the entire Euphrates basin lay within the southern Mesopotamian sphere of influence. [For a different view see above, 1.2. –Editor's note.]

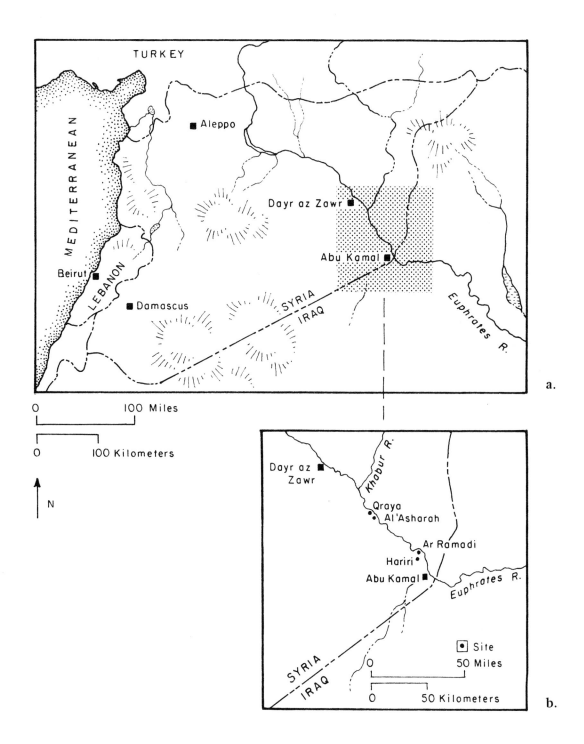

Figure 1a. Map of Syria.
Figure 1b. The region of Qraya.

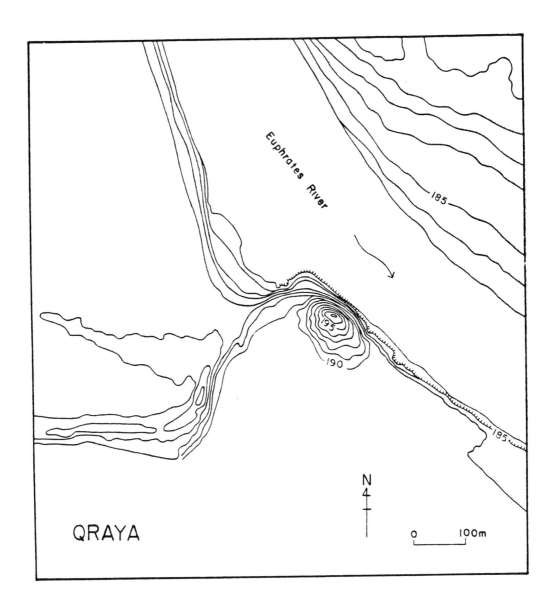

Figure 2.   Location of Tell Qraya.

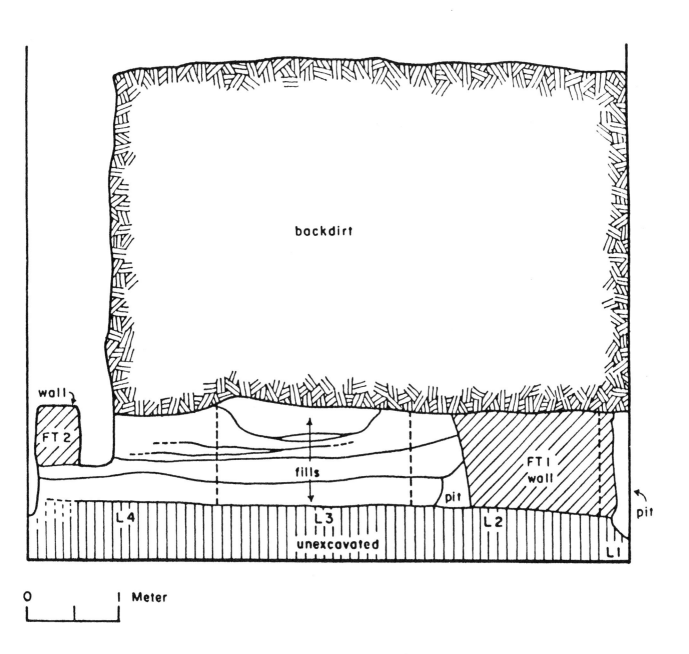

Figure 3.   QR1, SG1: Northwestern section.

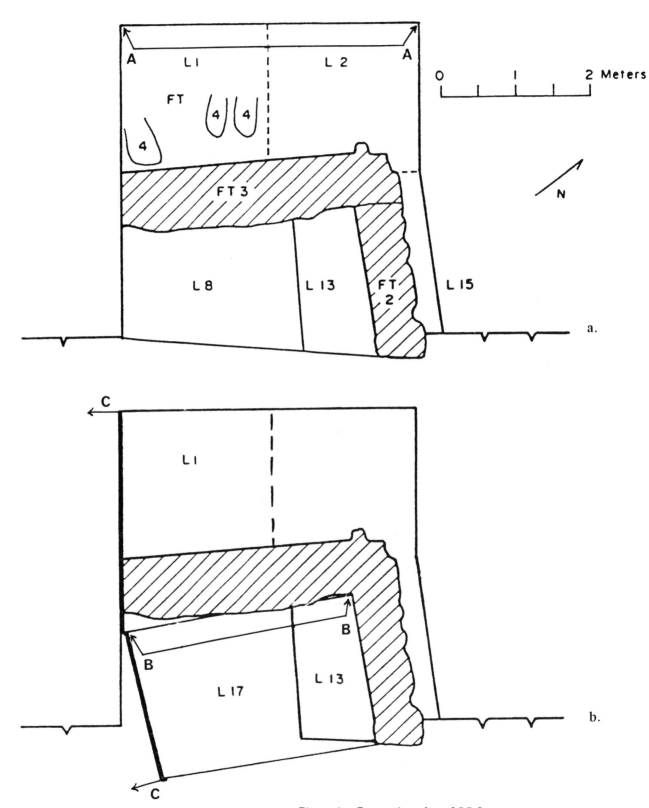

Figure 4.   Excavation plan of SG 2.
            a.   QR1 and QR2 field seasons.
            b.   QR3 field season.
(KEY: FT = Feature;   L = Locus)

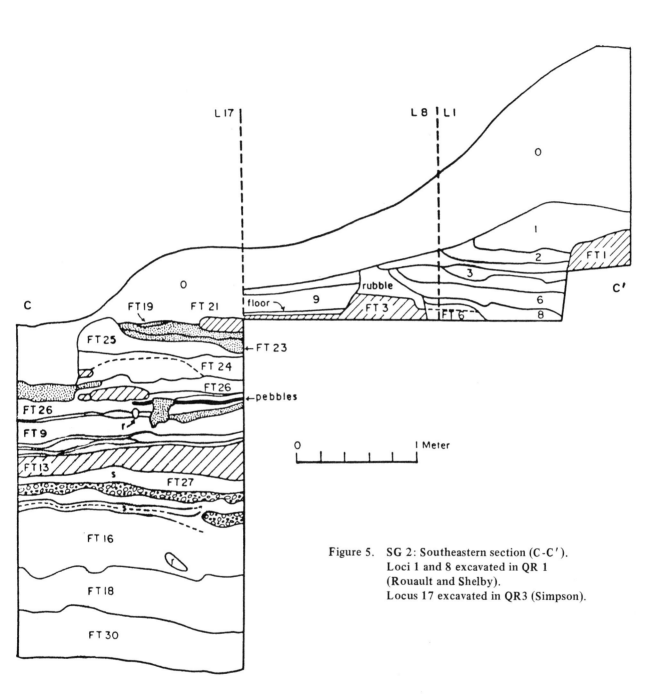

Figure 5. SG 2: Southeastern section (C-C').
Loci 1 and 8 excavated in QR 1
(Rouault and Shelby).
Locus 17 excavated in QR3 (Simpson).

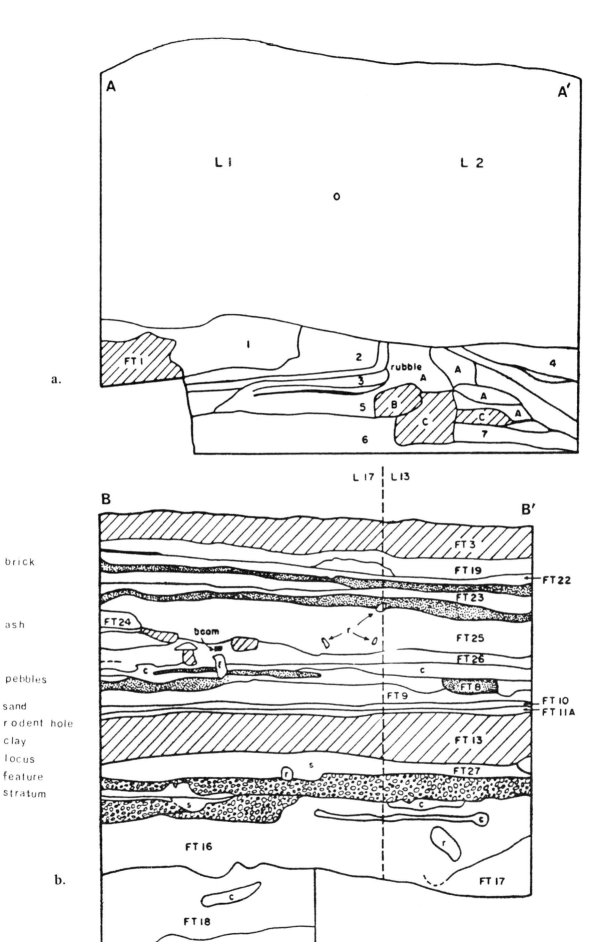

A   A'

L 1   L 2

o

a.

FT 1   1   2   rubble A   4
3   A
5   B   A   A
C   C   A
6   7

L 17 | L 13

B   B'

FT 3
FT 19
FT 22
FT 23
FT 24   beam   r   FT 25
f   FT 26
c   c   FT 8
FT 9   FT 10
FT 11A
FT 13
FT 27
s   r   c
s   c
r
FT 16
FT 17
c
FT 18
FT 30

	= brick
	= ash
	= pebbles
s	= sand
r	= rodent hole
c	= clay
L	= locus
FT	= feature
1-9	= stratum

b.

0   1 Meter

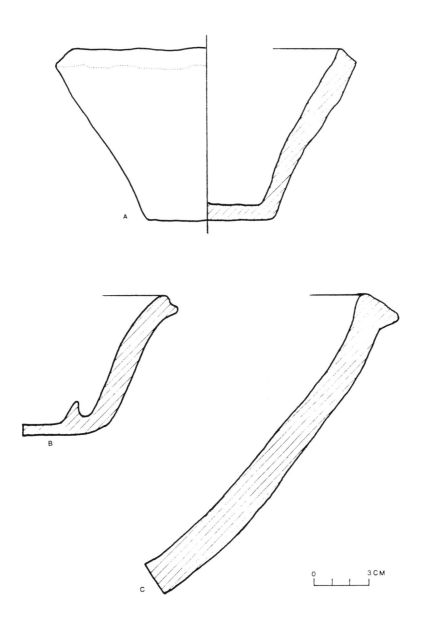

Figure 7.   Beveled rim and ledge rim bowl types of the Uruk period, Tell Qraya.

DESCRIPTION	REFERENCES
a beveled rim bowl – rim to base profile	
b beveled rim bowl – rim to base profile	Johnson 1973:Pl.I:a
c ledge rim, large bowl – rim	Surenhagen 1978:Tab.20:39

Figure 6.   SG 2: Northwest sections (A-A′ and B-B′).
a.   Loci 1 and 2 excavated in QR1 (Rouault and Shelby).
b.   Locus 13 excavated in QR2 (Simpson), and Locus 17 excavated in QR3 (Simpson).

Figure 8.   Miscellaneous bowl types of the Uruk period, Tell Qraya.
Key to Ceramic Types Illustrated

	DESCRIPTION	REFERENCES
a	flat based, deep bowl, thin ware – rim to base profile	Sürenhagen 1978:Tab.1:11
b	incised straight rim bowl – rim	
c	carinated round rim bowl – rim	Sürenhagen 1978:Tab.20:16
d	beveled rim bowl – rim	Sürenhagen 1978:Tab.20:24
e	direct rim, round lip bowl – rim	Sürenhagen 1978:Tab.20:27
f	flared rim bowl – rim	Sürenhagen 1978:Tab.22B:88
g	straight sided bowl – rim	Sürenhagen 1978:Tab.23:12
h	round rim bowl – rim	Johnson 1973:Pl.II:a; Sürenhagen 1978:Tab.22B:79
i	flat rim bowl, red ware – rim	Johnson 1973:Pl.II:g; Sürenhagen 1978:Tab.20:18
j	inverted rim bowl, red ware – rim	Sürenhagen 1978:Tab.20:10
k	carinated round rim bowl – rim	Sürenhagen 1978:Tab.20:13
l	tray, chaff tempered – rim to base profile	Johnson 1973:Pl.I:c; Sürenhagen 1978:Tab.23:11; Nissen 1972:Fig.37:087/13

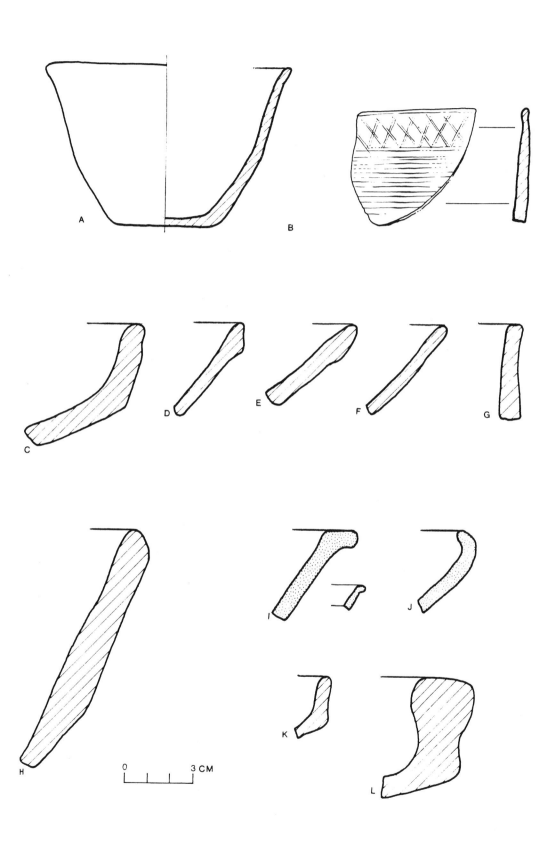

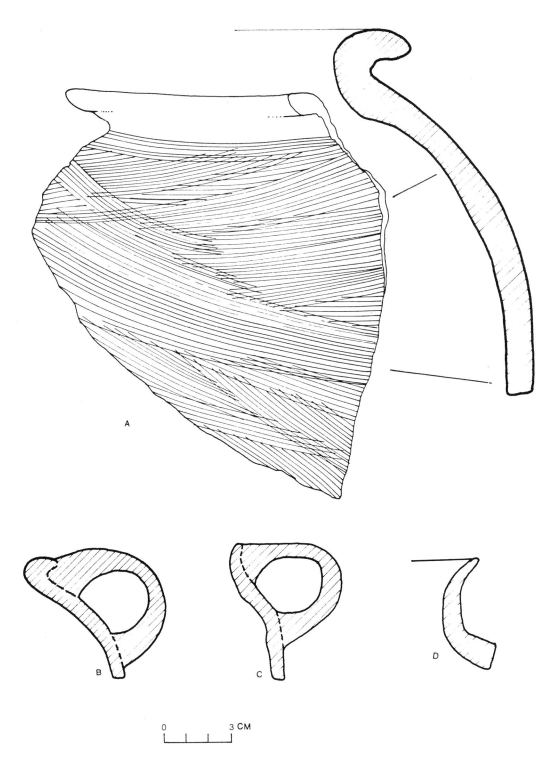

Figure 9.   Jar handles and jar rims of the Uruk period, Tell Qraya.

DESCRIPTION	REFERENCES
a outturned expanded rim jar with combing on body – rim	Johnson 1973:Pl.III:g; Pl.IV:f
b strap handed jar, ledge rim – rim	Johnson 1973:Pl.VII
c strap handed jar, rounded rim – rim	Sürenhagen 1978:Tab.33:1
d flared, high-necked jar – rim	Sürenhagen 1978:Tab.30:12

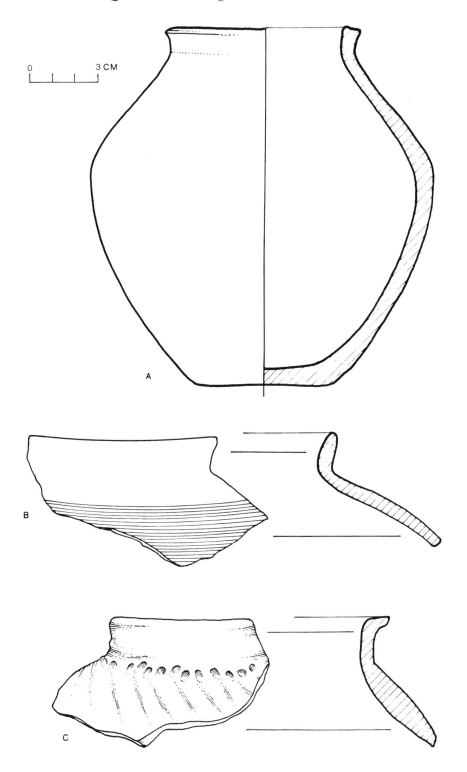

Figure 10. Miscellaneous jar types of the Uruk period, Tell Qraya.

DESCRIPTION	REFERENCES
a	flat-based, outcurving rim ovoid jar — rim to base profile	
b	flared round rim jar with incised lines on body — rim	Sürenhagen 1978:Tab.24:22
c	reserve slip and punctate jar shoulder — rim	Johnson 1973:Pl.IV:a; Nissen 1972:Fig.37:087/1

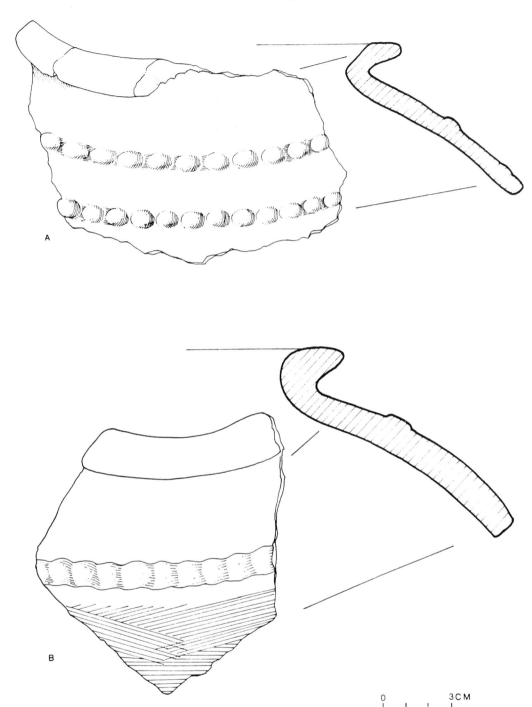

Figure 11. Decorated jar types of the Uruk period, Tell Qraya.

	DESCRIPTION	REFERENCES
a	outturned expanded rim jar with impressed strip – rim	Johnson 1973:Pl.II:d; Pl.III:g; Sürenhagen 1978:Tab.27:96
b	outturned expanded rim jar with impressed strip on shoulder and combing on lower body – rim	Johnson 1973:Pl.II:b, Pl.III:g; Pl.IV:f

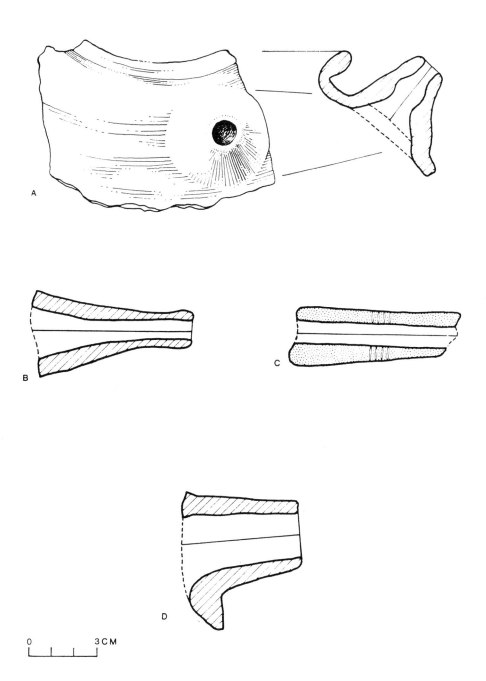

Figure 12. Spout types of the Uruk period, Tell Qraya.

	DESCRIPTION	REFERENCES
a	conical spouted jar with bands of incised lines − rim	Johnson 1973:Pl.VI:b; Sürenhagen 1978:Tab.27:96
b	straight spout	Johnson 1973:Pl.V:d; Sürenhagen 1978:Tab.33:G2
c	straight spout, incised red ware	
d	conical spout	Johnson 1973:Pl.VI:b; Sürenhagen 1978:Tab.33:G6

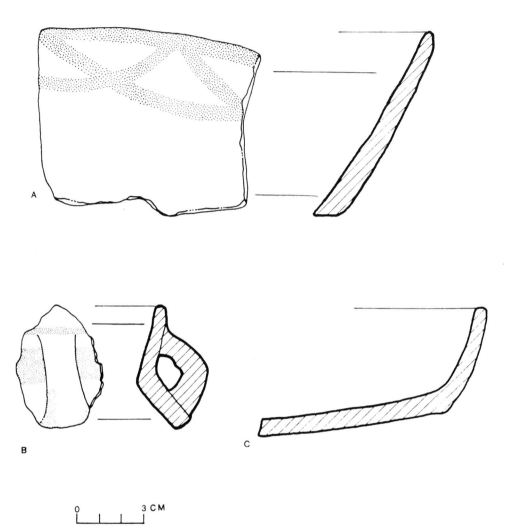

Figure 13. Ceramic types of the Ubaid period, Tell Qraya.

	DESCRIPTION	REFERENCES
a	round rim plate with brown paint on interior – rim	Nissen 1972:Fig.60; 267/5
b	jar handle, brown paint	
c	straight-sided deep plate, FF ware – rim to base profile	

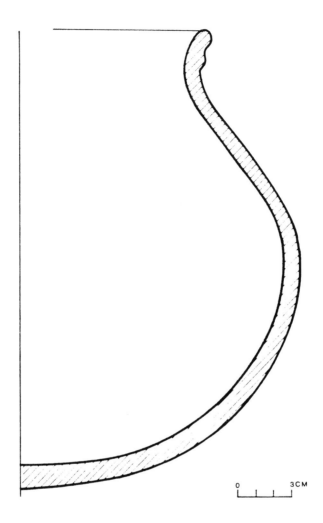

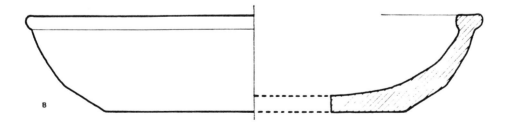

Figure 14. Ceramic types of the Old Babylonian period, Tell Qraya.

DESCRIPTION	REFERENCES
a small ovoid jar — rim to base profile	Kelly-Buccellati and Shelby 1977: Fig.12:TPR 4 23
b platter — rim to base profile	Kelly-Buccellati and Shelby 1977: Fig.9:TPR 4 13

3. References

Abu Al-Soof, Bahnam
    1985   *Uruk Pottery: Origin and Distribution.* Baghdad: State Organization of Antiquities
            and Heritage.

Adams, Robert McC.
    1965   *Land Behind Baghdad: A History of Settlement on the Diyala Plains.* Chicago:
            University of Chicago Press.

Adams, Robert McC., and Hans Nissen
    1972   *The Uruk Countryside: The Natural Setting of Urban Societies.* Chicago: University
            of Chicago Press.

Beale, Thomas W.
    1978   Bevelled Rim Bowls and Their Implications for Change and Economic Organization
            in the Later Fourth Millennium B.C. *Journal of Near Eastern Studies* 37:289-313.

Buccellati, Giorgio
    1977   The "Urban Revolution" in a Socio-Political Perspective. *Mesopotamia* 12:19-39.

    1979   Terqa Preliminary Reports, No. 10. The Fourth Season: Introduction and the
            Stratigraphic Record. *Bibliotheca Mesopotamica* 10. Malibu: Undena Publications.

Buccellati, Giorgio, and Beatrice Hopkinson
    forthc. Salt at the Dawn of History: The Case of the Bevelled Rim Bowls. In M. Van Loon,
            P. Matthiae, and H. Weiss (eds.), forthcoming.

Buccellati, Giorgio, and Marilyn Kelly-Buccellati
    1977   General Introduction and the Stratigraphic Record of the First Two Seasons.
            Syro-Mesopotamian Studies 1(3).

    1978   Terqa Preliminary Reports, No. 6. The Third Season: Introduction and the
            Stratigraphic Record. *Syro-Mesopotamian Studies* 2:115-64, Pls. I-XIV.

Bunnens, Guy
    1982   Sumer Outside of Sumer: Belgian Excavations at Tall Qannas, Syria. Paper presented
            March 5, Dept. of Anthropology, University of Arizona.

Delougaz, Pinhas
    1952   *Pottery from the Diyala Region.* Oriental Institute Publications 6 3. Chicago:
            University of Chicago Press.

Dyson, Robert H., Jr.
    1965   Problems in the Relative Chronology of Iran, 6000-2000 B.C. In R. W. Ehrich (ed.),
            Chronologies in Old World Archaeology, pp. 215-56. Chicago: University of Chicago
            Press.

Galvin, Kathleen F.
  1981   Early State Economic Organization and the Role of Specialized Pastoralism: Terqa in the Middle Euphrates Region, Syria. Ph.D. dissertation, University of California, Los Angeles.

Hansen, Donald P.
  1965   The Relative Chronology of Nippur from the Middle Uruk to the End of the Old Babylonian Period (3400-1600 B.C.). In R. W. Ehrich (ed.), *Chronologies in Old World Archaeology*, pp. 200-13. Chicago: University of Chicago Press.

Hopkinson, Beatrice
  1975   The Archaeological Evidence of Salt Moulding at Important European Salt Sites and Its Relationship to the Distribution of Urn-fielders. *Journal of Indo-European Studies* 3:1-52.

Johnson, Gregory A.
  1973   Local Exchange and Early State Development in Southwestern Iran. Ann Arbor: University of Michigan Museum of Anthropology, *Anthropology Papers* 51.

Kalsbeek, J.
  1980   La ceramique de serie du Djebel 'Aruda (a l'epoque d'Uruk). *Akkadica* 20:1-11.

Kelly-Buccellati, Marilyn, and William R. Shelby
  1977   A Typology of Ceramic Vessels of the Third and Second Millennia from the First Two Seasons. *Syro-Mesopotamian Studies* 1(6).

Kupper, J.-R.
  1950   *Correspondance de Kibri-Dagan, gouverneur de Terqa, ARMT 3*. Paris: Imprimerie Nationale.

Le Breton, L.
  1957   The Early Periods at Susa: Mesopotamian Relations. *Iraq* 19:79-124.

Lloyd, Seton
  1938   Some Ancient Sites in the Sinjar District. *Iraq* 5:123-42.

  1948   Uruk Pottery. *Sumer* 4:39-51.

Musil, Alois
  1927   *The Middle Euphrates: A Topographic Itinerary*. New York: American Geographical Society.

Nissen, Hans J.
  1972   Analysis of Archaeological Surface Collections. In R. McC. Adams and H. J. Nissen, *The Uruk Countryside*, pp. 95-218. Chicago: University of Chicago Press.

Nöldeke, Arnold, E. Heinrich, H. Lenzen, and A. V. Haller
  1932   *Vierter voläufiger Bericht über die von der Notgemeinschaft der Deutschen Wissenschaft in Uruk unternommenen Ausgrabungen*. Berlin: Abhandlungen der Preussischen Akademie der Wissenschaften.

Perkins, Ann Louise
    1949   *The Comparative Archaeology of Early Mesopotamia.* Studies in Ancient Oriental
           Civilization 25. Chicago: University of Chicago Press.

Shelby, William R.
    1978   Preliminary Notes on the Ceramics from Qraya. Ms. in possession of the author.

Shimabuku, D.
    1976   Possible Prehistoric System of Weight and Measures. Paper delivered at the 7th
           International Congress of Iranian Art and Archaeology, Munich.

Simpson, Kay
    1983   Settlement Patterns on the Margins of Mesopotamia: Stability and Change along the
           Middle Euphrates, Syria. Ph.D. dissertation, University of Arizona.

Sürenhagen, Dietrich
    1978   *Keramik-produktion in Habuba-Kabira-Sud: Untersuchungen zur Keramik-
           produktion innerhalb der Spät-Urukzeitlichen Siedlung Habuba Kabira-Süd in
           Nordsyrien.* Berlin: Verlag Brune Hessung.

Wright, Gary A.
    1969   Obsidian Analysis and Prehistoric Near Eastern Trade: 7500-3500 B.C. Ann Arbor:
           University of Michigan Museum of Anthropology, *Anthropology Papers* 37.

Wright, Henry T.
    1969   The Administration of Rural Production in an Early Mesopotamian Town. Ann
           Arbor: University of Michigan Museum of Anthropology, *Anthropology Papers* 38.